MARRIAGE MEDICINE VOLUME 7

"Decree It Until You See It"

MARRIAGE MEDICINE VOLUME 7

"Decree It Until You See It"

JESSICA SELVY-DAVIS

PO Box 1212 West Memphis, AR 72303

ISBN: 978-1-71664-814-4

DEDICATION

THIS STRATEGIC MARRIAGE MEDICINE VOLUME IS DEDICATED TO YOU...YES YOU! I BELIEVE IN YOU. YOU HAVE WHAT IT TAKES TO SHIFT THINGS FOR THE BETTER WITH YOUR WORDS. ALL IT TAKES IS FOR YOU TO RISE UP AND SPEAK UP!!

LIFE AND DEATH IS IN THE POWER OF YOUR TONGUE, THEREFORE WHAT YOU SEE IS WHAT YOU SAY ACCORDING TO MARK 11:23. YOU ARE EQUIPPED FOR IT AND MUST REFUSE TO LET THE DEVIL ROB YOU OF IT!!

TABLE OF CONTENTS

FOREWORD

I am honored to write this foreword and excited about how many people will be blessed by the prophetic insight and practical tools that are reflected in this volume of Marriage Medicine, released by my sister Prophetess Jessica Davis. I met this amazing woman of God years ago at church when she was dating my brother-in-love Apostle Jonathan Davis. As soon as I saw her with that big beautiful smile, I just knew that God had answered my prayers and that I was on the path to having a new sister and my brother-in-love would be blessed beyond measure to have her as his wife. Over the years, I have grown to know more about the anointing on her life to minster to the people of God. There are so many reasons that I believe Prophetess Jessica has been given this mandate and one of them is her love for the people of God. She has been gifted to teach on marriage principles that promote healthy and whole covenant marriages. This is such an authentic grace she has been blessed with that is poured out generously for the Body of Christ.

In this book, every prayer and principle released is a tool that can be used to do spiritual warfare and catapult your marriage into new depths in God. Every declaration will begin to water the new seeds that you are now planting in your marriage and you will begin to see those positive words shift your perception and begin to raise the level of expectancy and faith that you have for your marriage. As you go through this volume, take the time to pause and truly listen to the Holy Spirit as He leads and guides you on this journey. You will get divine instructions and gain considerable insight into your marriage. You will be able to navigate what God has placed in your hands to nurture, support, speak over, prophecy to, affirm, and love.

As you read this volume of Marriage Medicine, you will be challenged, enriched, edified, and strengthened by every chapter of this book. Allow the Holy Spirit to speak to you as you go on this journey of healing and restoration as a covenant partner with your spouse. Whatever you may be facing in your marriage, just know that you are in the right place at the right time. You will begin to see and experience the fruit of your labor. According to Hebrews 11:1, “Now faith is the substance of things hoped for and the evidence of things not seen.” So, move in faith as you take your daily prescription of Marriage Medicine. This will be an amazing adventure that you will not regret embarking upon.

Prophetess Marcia Ublies, MBA
(married to Norman Ublies -22 years)

INTRODUCTION

Marriage is a living organism. What you put into it is what it becomes. It must be taken care of and natured in order for it to blossom and grow. One of the main ways to make sure your marriage grows and evolves is to decree over it on a constant basis. It's true, watering your marriage with strategic word filled prayers will produce a healthy harvest in your relationship. So, Marriage Medicine Volume 7 "Decree It Until You See It" is your opportunity to say what you want to see.

It is time to call those things you want to happen in your marriage into being. Everything in this world was spoken into existence by the living word of God. Proverbs 18:21 states that "Life and death are in the power of your tongue." We live at the level in which we speak. It is time to speak life over every dead situation in your marriage. Some of us are reaping in our marriage that which was spoken out of our very mouth. Stop speaking things in the atmosphere that you don't want to manifest in your marriage. If you don't want a divorce, why are you talking about it? It's time to speak life into your marriage. Let's begin!
Allow me to start with speaking this prophetic decree and blessing over your marriage relationship:

In the name of Jesus, I decree that you are blessed in your marriage relationship. I decree that you have a close, covenant friendship with the husband/wife who loves you and is willing to die for you. I decree that you also love with the selfless, agape love of Jesus, and that you would also be willing to die for them. I release the heart of God into you right now. I decree that you are filled with the fullness of God's love right now, that you are able to love yourself like God loves you, love God back with all your heart, and love His people. I bless you with the ability to see people with His eyes and hear them with His ears. I decree that you have grace to love and honor your spouse, no matter what.
I decree that God's love must exude from every pore and fiber of your being into your marriage. I decree courage and boldness into you to evolve when the Father desires you to do so. I decree that you will be a place of safety, comfort, encouragement, and refuge to your spouse. I

decree that you have the ability to ask your spouse about themselves and truly care about the answers.

I decree in Jesus' name that you have a heart to serve, honor, and protect. I decree that you are trusted AND trustworthy. I decree that you have a heart to love your spouse unconditionally.
Husbands, I decree that you are equipped to love your wife as Christ loves the Church, being willing to give even your very life for her. Wives, I decree that you are able to love and submit to your husband as to the Lord.

Singles who desire to be married, I decree that you and your spouse will meet at the right time and in the right way. I call forth the godly, covenant marriage the Father desires you to have, and I command it to manifest in the Father's time and perfect will in Jesus' name. I decree that you have the patience in waiting. I decree that you will wait with a spirit of purity. I decree that you shall be holy, as God is holy; for without holiness, no man can see the Lord. I call forth the absolute fullness of godly relationships that Jesus Christ paid the price for you to have.
I speak to every new covenant the Father desires you to develop, and I command the plot of the enemy to be destroyed right now in Jesus' name.

CHAPTER ONE

"DECREE OVER DRASTIC CHANGES"

There's been a drastic life change for one or both of you; the severe illness or death of a child, chronic, serious health problems, financial issues like bankruptcy, loss of a job, loss of a parent or becoming a caretaker for a parent. Sure these drastic life changes can fight against your marriage immunity but you must make sure speaking the word of the Lord during this time is as important as the other priorities in your life.

DECREE: I decree that my marriage is based on a secure and solid foundation of God's Word. I will stand firm and not allow my shifting feelings or emotions to deter me. I will not compare, fantasize, complain, murmur, or belittle my spouse during difficult times. I declare that our family's future is blessed by God and will bring him glory and honor because I will approach the throne of grace with boldness, so that we may receive mercy and find grace to help us in time of need according to Hebrews 4:16.

CHAPTER TWO

"DECREE OVER NONVERBAL COMMUNICATION"

You used to have a great relationship and now your spouse won't talk to you. You feel distant from one another due to issues. It is true that relationships ebb and flow and in order to keep it strong, you need to change and flow with it. But you have to keep communicating to do that.

If either you or your partner has "clammed up" and won't talk about what's going on for any length of time, it can certainly lead to the end of the marriage. It's vital to be honest with yourself and with your spouse about what you are experiencing without blaming each other. You have one common enemy and it's miscommunication.

DECREE: I decree the cleansing blood of Jesus to erase any shame, any selfishness, any rebellion, and/or any unforgiveness I hold over my spouse that blocks me from communicating effectively. I decree freedom and liberty to come to my marriage. It is no longer held captive by the powers of disagreement, discord, deception and/or distance between us. I decree pure thoughts, pure motives, and pure words will be declared over my marriage and the shield of God's presence to cover and be established deep within our hearts according to Ephesians 4:2, "with all humility and gentleness, with patience, showing tolerance for one another in love."

CHAPTER THREE

"DECREE OVER ADULTERY/INFIDELITY"

You or your spouse had or is having an affair and there are serious trust issues. Trust issues, especially from past infidelity, can completely erode a relationship, let alone affairs that continue to go on. I encourage you to get clear about what you want and what you and your spouse's commitments are to your marriage. If you're tempted by an affair, even an emotional one, focus your attention on your God given mate instead to rediscover what's there. Readjust your focus towards making this relationship better with decreeing the word of truth. If you need extra help, I advise you to seek out wise counsel on concrete ways to build trust back in your relationship after cheating has occurred.

DECREE: I decree a renewed and deepened love for us and for the love of God to protect our marriage. I decree that no weapon formed against my marriage will prosper. I decree the full armor of God surrounding him/her throughout this day. I decree righteousness in my marriage and that truth and the promise of purity will be forever sealed. Our sex life is vibrant, passion filled, and pure. My mind & body are committed to my spouse and I yield my whole self to an intimate and unified perfect love with my husband/wife. I decree that our love is perfect and we are bound together by God's perfect love according to Hebrews 13:4, "Give honor to marriage, and remain faithful to one another in marriage. God will surely judge people who are immoral and those who commit adultery."

CHAPTER FOUR

"DECREE OVER ADDICTIONS"

Do you or your spouse have addictions that interfere with your marriage connection? Are you or your husband/wife numbing yourselves by using addictive substances? It's very difficult, if not impossible, to have a healthy relationship depending on the severity of the addiction. If addictions are keeping you and your loved one apart, get the help you need from a professional. Don't turn a blind eye to what's happening or make excuses. It usually only gets worse. Take control of the negativity by opening up your mouth to decree what you want to see positively.

DECREE: I decree a blessing over my marriage and declare that healing, prosperity, peace and joy will be our portion. I decree that my marriage is God-ordained and has a purpose for God's Kingdom.

I declare and decree that wicked patterns and cycles of addictions in my bloodline are over. I turn away from everything in my life and around me that gives Satan the power and legality to attack my marriage through addictions. Satan you have no power over my marriage because you did not create it. It was created by God and it is blessed by him according to Corinthians 10:13, "No temptation has overtaken you that is not common to man." God is faithful, and he will not let you be tempted beyond your ability, but with the temptation he will also provide the way of escape, that you may be able to endure it.

CHAPTER FIVE

"DECREE OVER ABUSE"

Are you experiencing emotional, verbal or physical abuse in your relationship? If there's violence of any kind in your marriage, don't make excuses for it because it's a call for help. The best advice I have is to take action quickly. A marriage filled with violence, even sporadic violence, is a demonic recipe for death and destruction. Thinking "YOU" alone can save him or her will never change things. Deliverance from God is needed to proceed healthily. If you are the victim, find a way to protection and pray until you know the violence has stopped forever. If you're the one prone to violence, pray for help now!! Don't excuse, justify or apologize your way through life. Take action to stop it.

DECREE: I come against every negative thought, action, deed, and word that was spoken to cause problems in my marriage, whether through me or my spouse. I decree that moving forward, we will do everything according to God's Word for our marriage to live. I revoke and resist every demonic assignment over our union and decree that we will be united together in love and spirit according to 2 Corinthians 10:3-5, "For though we walk in the flesh, we are not waging war according to the flesh. For the weapons of our warfare are not of the flesh but have divine power to destroy strongholds." We destroy arguments and every lofty opinion raised against the knowledge of God, and take every thought captive to obey Christ.

CHAPTER SIX

"DECREE OVER APATHY AND BOREDOM"

Maybe one or both of you are apathetic or bored in your relationship and it's the reason you are experiencing weakness in your marriage. This is the silent killer that creeps into relationships and usually the two people don't realize it's happened before it's too late. If you feel this might be happening in your relationship, tune into God and allow him to show you what's missing and how to communicate what you want. Decrees will breathe life into the areas in you that no longer feels alive. Remember you have to let God breathe life into you before you can revitalize your relationship with your spouse.

DECREE: I decree that Intimate Fire in our marriage shall grow, expand and flow like a mighty river. I decree that we are rooted and grounded in God's love and every ungodly voice over my marriage be silenced now, in the name of Jesus. I stand against the spirit of commonness and complacency. I take a stand against wondering eyes and decree that our love and intimacy will increase as the days go by, that we will always crave each other and no one else according to Philippians 2:3-4, "Do nothing out of selfish ambition or vain conceit, but in humility consider others better than yourselves." Each of you should look not only to your own interests, but also to the interests of others.

CHAPTER SEVEN

"DECREE OVER PAST PAIN"

One or both of you can't heal after the pain of a previous relationship breakup or divorce? We all carry unresolved emotions from previous relationships and many times, they are worked out in the new relationship. However, when the pain of the past interferes with the new relationship or when one of you lives more in the past than in the present, it can steal, kill and destroy the marriage. It's possible to come into the present moment and let the pain of the past move through you and dissolve. It can be a complex process but you can learn to see life differently if you choose.

DECREE: I decree that all Pain, Bitterness, Anger, Unforgiveness, Hurt, Hatred, Sorrow And Wounds festering in my marriage from past relationships is cleansed by the blood of Jesus and the balm of Gilead is releasing healing now to every place. I decree that the scent of my marriage shall be a pleasing aroma in your sight Lord and in the body of Christ. I decree that old wounds from our past will not cause infection in our present henceforth destroying our future according to Jeremiah 29:11, "For I know the plans I have for you, declares the Lord, "plans to prosper and not to harm you plans to give you a hope and a future."

CHAPTER EIGHT

"DECREE OVER BLENDED FAMILIES"

Many, but not all, remarriages involve blended families. Research shows that about 75 percent of 1.2 million Americans who divorce each year eventually remarry. Most have children and they find that stepfamily life is more complex than they ever imagined. It's full of complicated schedules, squabbling stepsiblings, issues with ex-partners, and new spouses who've never been parents trying out childcare. In the end, the most comforting piece of advice about blending families is this: A blended family is a family, first and foremost. The more you pray through the parenting experiences you gain, the more mistakes you make and learn from, the better you become at being a parent, stepparent, and spouse. The result? A healthier and happier well-adjusted blended family. Finally, but most important, effective parent-stepparent teams begin with healthy marriages. Take time to nurture your relationship, date on a regular basis, learn to communicate and resolve conflict, and enjoy a healthy sexual relationship. Make your marriage a priority!

DECREE: I raise the banner and the standard of Christ and declare the Lordship of Jesus over my marriage and family in the name of Jesus. I decree that my marriage shall bear good fruits and every Spirit of fear, favoritism and feuding is broken, and destroyed by the power of the blood of Jesus in my marriage and family. I decree that we have courage to build new relationships, the willingness to adjust to one another's habits, likes, and dislikes, and an ability to laugh over small things. Help us grow in love of one another, as you love us according to Colossians 2:2, "that their hearts may be encouraged, being knit together in love, to reach all the riches of full assurance of understanding and the knowledge of God's mystery, which is Christ."

CHAPTER NINE

"DECREE OVER FINANCES"

What if there is a time when you're not in the enviable position of being financially stable? What if one of you still has student loans or credit card debt to pay off? Mixing debts and uncertain jobs makes marriage even more fragile. You will need much self-discipline, however, to keep strained finances from starting quarrels and poisoning your relationship. The complicated thing about money in a marriage is that it's often tied up with power. We may believe that the person who makes the most money is more valued or should have the greater say in financial decisions. We need to remember that spouses perform many tasks for which they are not paid. They contribute to the marriage and common life in different ways. At times one spouse may be ill or unemployed and not able to contribute financially or in other ways. Spouses need to feel valued and respected in their own home, regardless of how much money they bring in. In a strong, life-giving marriage, financial responsibility is not just about making money and spending it or saving it. It also includes tithing, sowing and decreeing the word of the Lord over it.

DECREE: I decree that we are good stewards of God's blessings. I decree that we will have a hunger and thirst for learning how to manage our finances God's way. I decree a holy inspiration, motivation, and perseverance as we dig into God's truth about finances. I decree that we are doers of the Word, and not hearers only. From this day forward, we will handle money God's way, and we will see with our own eyes the blessings we are receiving and the progress we are making in our finances. I decree that we will have a mentality of abundance starting today. I decree that my spirit, soul, and body are all open to receive the fullness of financial prosperity from the Father. I decree and release blessings into our home right now in Jesus' name. I decree that, from this day forward, we are blessed financially. I decree from this day forward that we shall prosper.

I decree surprise financial blessings, surprise gifts, surprise donations, surprise discounts, surprise checks in the mail, and good surprises in every part of our finances because we work the principles of giving. I decree that our business(s) prospers, that we have at least 8 various streams of income and that we have favor everywhere we go, and that we are radically generous givers. I decree that we have plenty of finances to do everything we need to do, plus more according to Deuteronomy 8:18, "And you shall remember the Lord your God, for it is

He who gives you power to get wealth, that He may establish His covenant which He swore to your fathers, as it is this day."

CHAPTER TEN

"DECREE OVER WAITING HUSBAND/WIFE"

It's never too soon to start praying for your future spouse, even if you don't know them yet. Whatever season of life you're in, you need to pray. We all do. Whether single and praying about your desire for a husband/wife, or later if you're married, praying about your desire for a baby, or praying for your (or your spouse's) need for a job, or if you never do marry, praying about serving faithfully while celibate, the need to pray never ends. Jesus told His disciples they "always ought to pray and not lose heart." It's never too soon, or too late, to start. God is able to bring you a husband/wife. But even more remarkably, if He doesn't right away, He is able to hold you fast and keep you trusting Him and believing that He is good.

DECREE: I call forth my marriage partner in the name of Jesus
Father contend with every contention at my gate of marriage. I decree that every deaf and dumb spirit that causes me not to see my spouse be destroyed by the Blood of Jesus. I decree that the fire of God burns away every hindrance that stands in the way of us connecting in the spirit. I decree that the power of Holy Ghost cast away the deaf and dumb spirit that causes my spouse not to see me, let it be destroyed in the name of Jesus. Cleanse my eyes with your eye salve that I may see my partner in the spirit and every wicked handwriting of ordinances over my marital status be blotted out by the blood of Jesus. Father open forth your armory and release your special weapons of warfare and wage war against the strongman that is standing at my gate of marriage. I decree that the enemy shall release my spouse from every imprisonment of the enemy now. The Blood of Jesus, your power, your majesty, your authority, your dominion let it take charge at my gate of marriage against every demonic declaration, utterance, covenant agreement and contract made out of ignorance. Be lifted in my life most powerful, and glorious master who will keep your promises according to 1 Thessalonians 5:25, "He who calls you is faithful; he will surely do it."

APPENDIX

Now that you know that your words have the power to produce change in your marriage, consider Proverbs 18:21 as a reminder: words kill, words give life; they're either poison or fruit. YOU CHOOSE!

The moment God revealed to me that marriage is the most valuable relationship on this side of heaven, I immediately wanted my words to be fruit rather than poison. It's my desire that the words that I speak bring life and build my marriage, rather than poison and tear it down. This year I celebrate 17 years of marriage and I've began focusing on how we could build it to last 100 plus more. I was reminded of something I learned several years ago from my grandmother and that was, the institution of marriage is one in which there is great contention, going into marriage, and staying in marriage there is great warfare. The devil has so invaded marriage that it may seem more attractive to stay outside of that great institution that was instituted by the Lord himself, but marriage is a blessing and ultimately brings God glory.

The words she spoke penetrated straight to my heart, leaving me contemplating how to proceed forward with what I had just learned. She taught me the power and importance of prayer over my husband and marriage. She modeled her daily routine that included confessing scripture and praying over specific areas for my grandfather each day. As I thought through how I could apply this powerful principle to growing my marriage, I found a few biblical confessions to declare over my marriage relationship every day and want to share with you to release over yours as well.

• My husband and I are one flesh and no one can tear that apart (Matthew 19:4-6).
• I am a crown for my husband's head. I bring him wisdom and honor all the days of my life (Proverbs 12:4).
• My husband and I stand together, united in Christ. We have each other's backs and operate as a team (Ecclesiastes 4:12).
• I submit to my husband as to the Lord. I respect him and honor him as

the head of our house (Ephesians 5:22-24).

- I am a fountain of blessing to my husband. We rejoice in each other (Proverbs 5:18-19).
- I am my husband's helper, a perfect fit for him (Genesis 2:18).
- I am precious and valuable to my husband and I continually add value to him (Proverbs 31:10).
- I accept the authority of my husband and clothe myself with the beauty that comes from within, the unfading beauty of a gentle and quiet spirit (1 Peter 3:1-3).
- I will fulfill my husband's sexual needs, laying down my rights to what I "feel" or "don't feel" like doing (1 Corinthians 7:3).
- I will intentionally love my husband in his love language, because love makes up for all offenses (Proverbs 10:12).
- I will give honor to my marriage and stay faithful to my husband (Hebrews 13:4).
- I will be patient and kind towards my husband and not boastful, rude or keep a record of his wrongdoings. I will never give up on him, but always cheer him on in faith (1 Corinthians 13:4-7).

Transparent Moment

These confessions are what I wanted to see in my marriage and truth is, you may not necessarily see the fruit right away. Don't get me wrong, I love my husband and we have a wonderful relationship. But just like everyone else, we are on a journey and if you want to improve in the areas where you're weak and the places where you know the enemy seeks to come in, you must use your mouth to exercise your faith in order to receive what you know God has promised. The more you confess these things, the more you believe them and stay committed to your covenant you will eventually get results. I pray that as you begin confessing these things over your lives that you will begin to see God's hand moving in your marriage. Bible says that the ear of the lord is not deaf nor his hand short that he does not hear us, but our iniquities have separated us from our God (paraphrased) Isaiah 59:1. We therefore must first bring repentance over our past participation by thoughts words or deed our iniquities which would cause the Lord not to hear us. Let us stand on this word for our marriage and believe that all things will work together for good to them that love the lord. That our marriages shall have the fragrance of the Lord, they shall be appealing both to us and to the onlookers, that our spouses will be goodly and Godly people, that our marriages shall be strong, fruitful and honorable in the sight of the Lord.

I want to share a final confession for your marriage that I love from Kenneth Copeland:

My marriage is blessed. My spouse and I are led by the Spirit of God. When we pray together in unity, our prayers are powerful and we get results. We make every effort to establish peace and harmony in our home. Together we walk in agreement and are an unstoppable force. If we get angry, we are quick to forgive so that we do not have strife in our relationship. We are not self-seeking, rude, proud, boastful, or jealous. Instead, we are loving, kind, patient and we put each other needs before our own. We trust each other and protect the sanctity of our marriage. God joined us together as one, and we will not be separated.

Scripture References: Deuteronomy 28:1-14, Romans 8:14, Matthew 18:19, I Peter 3:7, Mark 11:25, Romans 13:13, I Corinthians 13:4-8, Matthew 19:6

REFERENCES

https://www.biblegateway.com/

https://www.givinglight.org/marriage-decrees/

https://www.afterwesayido.com/prayer-declarations-over-your-marriage-bydauren-francis/

https://www.fromhispresence.com/prophetic-decree-4-fullness-of-relationships/

https://www.biblestudytools.com/bible-verse-of-the-day/

https://www.keepinspiring.me/marriage-quotes/

ABOUT THE AUTHOR

Prophet Jessica Selvy-Davis is Co-Pastor and Co-Founder of Kingdom Seekers International Ministry of Arts, where she serves in ministry alongside her husband, Apostle Jonathan Davis. She is a woman who God has graced and gifted with many anointings, and she moves in them fluently and with excellence. She is an Intercessor, Mentor, Praise and Worship Leader, Author, Midwife and a Mother of many.

Prophet Jessica is fueled with a passion to advance God's Kingdom and to make His name praised in the earth. Known for her wit and sense of humor, she ministers effectively to the heart of God's people. She has a tender heart for women. She desires women to break out of the box of limitations and expand their horizon to pursue purpose and destiny. She is valued for her wisdom and intellect, and her integrity is sound. Prophet Jessica governs in the earth realm, and is determined to fulfill every prophetic word spoken over her to carry out the spiritual mandate that God has placed in her hands. She is a native of West Memphis, AR, where she serves faithfully for God's glory.

To request Prophet Jessica Selvy-Davis for speaking engagements, please email: kingdomseekers_ministryofarts@hotmail.com.

To send comments or questions please message her via
Email: lenoraselvy@yahoo.com
Facebook: https://www.facebook.com/100004940706891

https://www.paypal.me/AuthorSelvyDavis

NOTES

NOTES

NOTES

www.ingramcontent.com/pod-product-compliance
Ingram Content Group UK Ltd.
Pitfield, Milton Keynes, MK11 3LW, UK
UKHW020137250726
13967UKWH00002B/705

9 781716 648144